AF688212

Frostfire Fortune

Frostfire Fortune

Matthew Petchinsky

1

Frostfire Fortune: Unlocking Winter's Hidden Prosperity
By: Matthew Petchinsky

Introduction

Cold stillness holds hidden abundance, waiting to be thawed.

Winter has always been a paradox. To the untrained eye, it is the season of endings—fields barren, rivers locked in ice, and silence blanketing the world in a frost that seems eternal. Yet beneath this stillness, the earth is not dead but storing. The soil is thick with seeds waiting for their appointed hour, rivers still flow beneath their frozen shells, and trees cradle sap deep in their cores, conserving strength until spring calls it forth. In this hush, prosperity sleeps, cloaked by frost.

Wealth, too, often hides in the coldest seasons of our lives. When resources seem frozen, when opportunities appear sealed away, and when the world feels motionless, abundance has not vanished—it has only gone into hiding. The secret lies in knowing how to thaw it, how to strike the balance between ice and fire, between patience and ignition.

This book, *Frostfire Fortune*, is your key to that hidden treasury. It does not treat winter as a time of scarcity, but as a chamber of secrets. Within these pages you will discover rituals that marry flame and frost, heat and stillness, to unseal prosperity waiting for release. Here, frozen wealth will be warmed into movement. Here, you will learn to draw strength from the season of frost, using its crystalline clarity to sharpen intention, while kindling inner fire to unlock action and manifestation.

Cold teaches restraint, clarity, and focus. Fire teaches drive, passion, and movement. Together, they are the alchemy of winter prosperity—the Frostfire current. By aligning with this current, you will see that winter is not the death of growth, but the forge of it. Your abundance is waiting beneath the ice. With the right rituals, the frost will crack, the flame will rise, and your fortune will flow free.

Chapter 1: The Icebound Wallet — Freezing Debt Through Ice Jars

Winter has always been a teacher in stillness. When the rivers freeze, the flow does not disappear—it simply waits. So too with money: the circulation of abundance can be slowed, redirected, or preserved. Debt is often energy that has grown wild—an obligation unbalanced, a tether draining your warmth. The secret is not to "kill" it but to freeze its movement, to still its draining pull so that you may regain command.

In this chapter, we turn to the **Ice Jar Rituals**—time-honored techniques of freezing harmful currents. These methods do not erase responsibility, but they halt the psychic, energetic, and spiritual bleed of debt. Once contained, your finances are freed from constant pressure, and your own flame of prosperity may rise without interruption.

Spell One: The Frozen Ledger
Purpose: To suspend the grip of lingering debts that feel oppressive.
Materials:

- A small glass jar with lid
- A slip of paper
- Pen with blue or black ink
- A pinch of salt
- Water

Method:

1. Write the names of all creditors, lenders, or bills that feel overwhelming on the slip of paper. Write them as clearly as possible.
2. Fold the paper three times toward you, sealing intent to bring the debt into your control.
3. Place the folded paper in the jar, adding a pinch of salt for purification.
4. Fill the jar halfway with water. As you pour, whisper: *"By frost, by stillness, I command this weight to pause."*
5. Seal the jar and place it in the freezer. Let it rest undisturbed.

Result: As the jar freezes, the psychic intensity of your debt is symbolically suspended. The pressure eases, allowing you to think clearly and plan repayment without panic or shame.

Spell Two: The Icebound Flame

Purpose: To bind reckless spending impulses that lead to further debt.

Materials:

- One tealight candle (red or gold)
- A small heat-safe bowl
- Water
- A coin or token representing money

Method:

1. Place the coin at the bottom of the bowl.
2. Fill the bowl with water until the coin is submerged.
3. Set the tealight carefully on the frozen surface after you place the bowl in the freezer for one night.
4. On the following evening, light the tealight on top of the ice, letting fire burn above frozen water.
5. Speak aloud: *"Fire above, ice below—reckless flow is bound and slowed."*

Result: The flame burns but does not melt through the ice quickly. This represents the balance of passion (fire) and restraint (ice). As the candle burns out, your impulses are cooled, and reckless spending loses its hold.

Spell Three: The Debt Frost Bind

Purpose: To symbolically trap debt collectors, interest, or late fees that spiral endlessly.

Materials:

- A strip of white cloth or ribbon
- Ice cubes (7 pieces)
- A small plastic bag

Method:

1. Write the word **"DEBT"** across the cloth. Beneath it, write the phrases: "Interest," "Fees," "Collectors."
2. Wrap each ice cube with a fold of the cloth, chanting: *"Frozen tight, bound by night, debt loses bite."*
3. Place the wrapped ice cubes into the plastic bag and seal it.
4. Put the bag in your freezer, letting it rest at the farthest corner.

Result: As the ice remains frozen, the influence of extra charges, collectors, or energy-draining fees symbolically halts. You create a protective pause, giving yourself space to pay only what is fair and necessary.

Meditation: The Frosted Vault

Purpose: To reprogram your inner wealth consciousness and visualize debt as frozen, powerless.

Practice:

1. Sit in silence, spine straight, hands resting gently on your knees.
2. Close your eyes and imagine a great vault of ice in front of you—its doors crystalline, shining blue.
3. One by one, see your debts as small slips of paper. Place them inside the vault. With each deposit, whisper: *"Frozen still, you hold no will."*
4. Seal the vault in your mind's eye. See frost sweep across the doors, locking them firmly shut.
5. Now, shift focus inward. Imagine a flame glowing in your chest, rising as the vault closes. See that the fire is yours—it is not diminished by the frozen vault, but liberated, able to grow without being drained.
6. Stay in this visualization for 7–10 minutes, breathing steadily.

Outcome: You emerge with the sense that your debts are no longer alive, clawing at you. They are paused, suspended, held in frost. Your fire of prosperity is free to expand, bringing solutions and opportunities into being.

Chapter 2: Frostfire Mindset — Meditating with Candle Over Ice

Prosperity is not summoned only through ritual objects or sacred words. It begins within the mind. Wealth is a current, and like water, it flows to the vessel best prepared to receive it. If the vessel is cracked by fear, scarcity, or frantic desire, abundance drains away before it can gather. To become a true keeper of prosperity, one must learn the **Frostfire Mindset**—a balance between the stillness of ice and the transformative power of flame.

Where ice teaches **patience, restraint, and clarity**, fire teaches **drive, transformation, and creation**. Together, they form a partnership: frost steadies the heart while flame fuels ambition. The practice of meditating with a candle placed above ice is an ancient symbolic method of awakening this dual mindset. It is simple, yet profound—because it unites opposites and teaches your spirit to hold tension without breaking.

The Symbolism of Candle Over Ice

- **The Candle Flame:** Represents your will, burning steadily in a world full of distractions. It is the spark of ambition, vision, and hunger for growth.
- **The Ice Base:** Represents grounding, patience, and the containment of reckless urges. It cools chaos, ensuring your fire does not consume all resources in a single burst.
- **Together:** The flame warms the ice slowly. The ice steadies the flame. You are trained to hold both states—discipline and passion, stillness and movement, winter and summer—inside yourself at once.

This is the heart of the Frostfire Mindset: to know when to burn and when to wait.

The Frostfire Meditation Ritual

Materials Needed:

- One thick glass bowl
- Ice cubes (enough to create a solid layer at the bottom of the bowl)
- One tealight or votive candle
- Matches or lighter
- A quiet, dim space

Preparation:

1. Place the ice cubes in the bowl, letting them settle into a smooth surface.
2. Set the candle directly on top of the ice. Ensure it is steady and will not tip.
3. Sit comfortably with the bowl before you, spine straight, hands relaxed on your knees.

Steps of the Practice:

1. **Lighting the Flame**
    - Light the candle, focusing on the ignition. Whisper: *"Flame of my will, rise."*
    - As the flame steadies, imagine your own determination taking shape with it.
2. **Witnessing the Balance**
    - Observe how the flame stands steady above the frozen surface.
    - Recognize this as a mirror of yourself: fire of drive standing upon the calmness of restraint.
3. **Breathing Frostfire**
    - Inhale deeply, imagining the coolness of ice filling your lungs. Feel it sharpen your awareness, clearing clutter from your mind.
    - Exhale slowly, picturing warmth leaving your chest and merging with the flame before you. Let your passion fuel the fire.
    - Continue this breath cycle for several minutes: inhale frost, exhale fire.
4. **Mind's Invocation**
    - As you breathe, repeat silently:
      "I hold stillness. I hold fire. In me, prosperity does not scatter—it gathers."
    - Feel the words root in your consciousness like seeds waiting to thaw.
5. **Closing the Practice**
    - When ready, snuff the candle (do not blow it out; pinch or cover it to seal the energy).
    - Allow the ice to melt naturally. As it returns to water, imagine your wealth channels flowing freely, unobstructed.

Three Mindset Spells to Anchor Prosperity

These are not separate rituals, but affirmations and micro-practices to reinforce the Frostfire state throughout your day.

1. The Frost Breath Pause

Whenever anxiety about money rises, stop. Inhale slowly through your nose as if breathing in the crisp chill of winter air. Hold it three seconds. Exhale with the words: *"Cold steadies me."* This cools emotional panic and restores clarity.

2. The Flame Spark Intention

Each morning, light a small candle and speak your single wealth goal aloud: "Today I move closer to [specific aim]." Extinguish it after a few minutes, carrying the spark within you all day.

3. The Balance Stone

Carry a small pebble in your pocket. When you feel pulled into extremes—spending recklessly, or hoarding fearfully—touch the stone and silently repeat: *"Frostfire holds me steady."* This anchors you to balance.

Guided Frostfire Visualization

Close your eyes and see yourself standing in a great frozen cavern. Before you lies a block of clear ice, within it a glowing ember. At first, the ember seems trapped. But as you place your hands upon the ice, you feel warmth radiate from your palms, not melting recklessly but slowly thawing a path. The ember grows brighter, until the whole cavern is filled with both cool crystalline light and warm golden fire.

This is you—your Frostfire Mindset. Wealth flows to one who can hold ice and fire in balance, never rushing blindly, never freezing permanently.

Chapter 3: Frozen Lake Offering — Summoning Gifts Through Reflection Rituals

Winter lakes appear silent, lifeless, sealed in glass. Yet anyone who has stood beside one knows the truth: beneath the surface, water still moves. Fish drift slowly in the cold, plants sleep under layers of frost, and currents of unseen life continue. The ice above acts as a mirror—reflecting the sky, reflecting yourself, reflecting what you choose to place before it.

In magick, reflection is not passive. It is a gateway. The frozen lake teaches us that prosperity often comes when we **offer our intent into stillness**, letting reflection magnify it and echo it back into the world. When you place a gift or symbol upon the ice, you summon a return. When you stare into the icy surface with purpose, the reflection becomes a contract between you and the unseen powers of abundance.

This chapter unveils the art of the **Frozen Lake Offering**, a series of reflection rituals to call wealth, opportunity, and generosity into your life.

The Meaning of Reflection Offerings

- **Mirror Principle:** What you show is returned. If you reflect poverty, the world amplifies it. If you reflect wealth, the lake echoes prosperity back.
- **Frozen Barrier:** Ice creates a veil. Your offering rests above, while the current below carries your request into deeper realms.
- **Symbol of Patience:** The lake does not rush to return your gift; it multiplies it in silence, teaching you to trust the unseen.

The Frozen Lake Offering Ritual

Materials Needed:

- A bowl or dish filled with water, frozen overnight (or a trip to a real frozen pond if safe)
- Three coins (silver or copper preferred)
- A white or silver candle
- A small piece of paper and pen

Steps:

1. **Prepare the Offering Surface**
    - Freeze a bowl of water until it forms a solid sheet of ice. Smooth the top if necessary. Place it on your altar or windowsill.
2. **Write Your Request**
    - On the slip of paper, write one gift you wish to summon: financial support, a specific opportunity, or a resource you need. Keep it simple.
3. **Place the Gifts**
    - Set the three coins in a triangle upon the ice. Place the folded paper at the center. Light the candle nearby so its flame reflects on the icy surface.
4. **Speak the Invocation**
    - Whisper: *"Frozen mirror, hold my plea. Reflect it back, return to me."* Repeat nine times, focusing on the paper glowing in candlelight.
5. **Seal the Offering**
    - Let the candle burn for 15 minutes, then extinguish it. Keep the ice with coins until it melts. Pour the water outside onto the earth, symbolizing the release of your request.

Result: Your offering is carried into the unseen channels of prosperity. Within days or weeks, a gift—material or unexpected—finds its way to you.

Three Spells for Reflection Abundance

1. The Mirror Coin Spell

- Place a single polished coin on frozen water (in a glass dish).
- Gaze at the coin's reflection, imagining it multiplying.
- Say: *"One becomes many, mirrored wealth returns."*
- Keep the coin in your wallet afterward as a magnet for money.

2. The Gift Echo Charm

- Hold a small wrapped item (stone, crystal, or trinket).
- Press it gently against frozen ice and whisper: *"What I give, returns with grace."*
- Leave the token outdoors or at a natural body of water. Expect reciprocity within a lunar cycle.

3. The Silver Thread Ritual

- Stretch a piece of silver or white ribbon across frozen ice.
- Imagine it as a bridge between your reflection and the world beneath.
- Chant: *"Thread of frost, thread of flame, bind abundance to my name."*
- Store the ribbon in a jar with herbs like basil or cinnamon for continued prosperity draw.

Meditation: Gazing Into the Ice Mirror

Purpose: To align your inner reflection with the wealth you wish to call forth.

1. Sit with a frozen bowl of water before you, candlelight shining upon it.
2. Gaze softly at the surface until your reflection begins to blur.
3. Imagine the "you" in the ice as the version of yourself who already holds abundance, security, and prosperity.
4. Ask silently: *"What gifts have you received? What did you become to receive them?"*
5. Listen for impressions, images, or sensations. The reflection-self becomes a guide, teaching you how to embody wealth now.
6. When complete, place your hand over the ice and whisper: *"As above, so reflected—so shall it be."*

Outcome: You leave with a sense of wholeness, clarity, and alignment. The reflection-self walks beside you in daily life, magnetizing gifts you once thought hidden.

Chapter 4: Snowstorm Spellcasting — Multiplying Fortune in Chaos

Snowstorms are nature's paradox: violent, disorienting, and blinding—yet life-giving. Beneath the fury of white chaos, the earth is nourished. Snow blankets fields, sealing in moisture and protecting roots. What looks destructive is often a hidden blessing.

In wealth magick, chaos can be treated the same way. Bills arrive unexpectedly, markets shift without warning, and opportunities seem to vanish in the whiteout of uncertainty. But chaos is also multiplication: countless flakes falling together to transform the land overnight. What seems like loss can conceal massive gain. The secret of **Snowstorm Spellcasting** is to embrace turbulence as raw material—channeling its power to multiply fortune rather than scatter it.

The Nature of Storm Fortune

- **Whiteout as Reset:** Storms erase old tracks, forcing new paths. Financially, chaos can clear stagnant debts or outdated plans, creating space for new streams of income.
- **Snowflake Principle:** Each flake seems small, but together they cover entire landscapes. Prosperity works the same—countless small actions and opportunities snowball into vast abundance.
- **Storm Current:** The whirling motion of a blizzard teaches us to summon and gather scattered wealth, pulling it inward to form a mound of fortune at our feet.

Spell One: The Blizzard Jar of Multiplication
Purpose: To summon multiplied streams of fortune from chaos.
Materials:

- A clear jar with lid
- Shredded white paper or snowflake confetti
- Silver glitter (to represent fortune in chaos)
- A small written note with your wealth request

Method:

1. Write your request for multiplied fortune (e.g., "income streams grow," "royalties expand," "unexpected gifts arrive").
2. Place the note in the jar, covering it with shredded paper and glitter.
3. Shake the jar vigorously while chanting:
   "From storm to storm, wealth is born.
   From scatter to gather, riches swarm."
4. Let the jar rest on your altar during a real storm, or place it in your freezer to keep the blizzard energy active.

Result: As the jar embodies storm chaos, it becomes a vortex of multiplication. Wealth begins arriving in clusters, often from unusual or hidden sources.

Spell Two: The Snowdrift Gathering

Purpose: To collect scattered wealth and opportunities into one mound, like a drift forming in wind.

Materials:

- A white cloth or napkin
- A handful of rice or sugar (representing snowflakes)
- A small magnet

Method:

1. Lay the cloth flat, sprinkling the rice/sugar across it.
2. Place the magnet at the center. Slowly fold the cloth inward, gathering the grains into a pile around the magnet.
3. As you do, say: *"All that scatters, gathers to me. Chaos, bind in prosperity."*
4. Store the magnet in your wallet or money box.

Result: Financial opportunities that once slipped away are drawn back, clustering together into wealth you can hold.

Spell Three: The Whiteout Debt Dissolver

Purpose: To symbolically obscure debts, fees, or financial burdens so they lose power.

Materials:

- A slip of paper with debts written on it
- A white candle
- A shallow dish filled with salt or powdered sugar

Method:

1. Place the paper in the dish, covering it completely with salt or sugar until it vanishes.
2. Light the white candle above the dish, saying: *"In storm's white veil, this burden fades. Chaos dissolves, fortune is made."*
3. Let the candle burn at least halfway, then snuff it. Keep the dish in a safe place until you feel financial relief. Then dispose of the contents outdoors.

Result: The energetic presence of debt is obscured, giving you freedom of spirit to focus on new inflows rather than old drains.

Meditation: Standing in the Storm

Purpose: To harness chaos without fear and redirect it toward multiplication.

1. Sit quietly with eyes closed. Imagine yourself in the center of a raging snowstorm. Winds whip around you, snow blinds your vision, and sound is muffled in the storm's roar.
2. Instead of resisting, breathe deeply into the stillness within your chest. Realize that the chaos cannot touch your inner flame.
3. See snowflakes swirling toward you, not away. Imagine them landing at your feet, piling up into a growing mound of silver-white light.
4. Whisper: *"All that scatters, gathers. Chaos is my wealth."*
5. Stay with the image of the growing mound until you feel its weight, then carry that sensation back into waking life.

Outcome: You emerge with the sense that what once overwhelmed you is now fuel. Every storm is wealth in disguise, every disordered current an opportunity to multiply.

Chapter 5: Flame on Ice — Igniting Opportunity Through Controlled Thawing

Ice is not an enemy; it is a guardian. It preserves, slows, and holds until the right time. Yet, abundance cannot remain locked forever. To prosper, frozen wealth must be released—but if it melts too quickly, it floods and is lost. This is why we practice **controlled thawing**, where flame and ice work together to release opportunity in careful, steady measure.

Just as spring comes gradually, not in one sudden blaze, so must your prosperity be thawed. By applying symbolic fire upon ice, you teach your spirit to welcome opportunities in a way that is manageable, balanced, and lasting. Controlled thawing ensures wealth is received with wisdom, rather than squandered in reckless heat.

The Lesson of Flame on Ice

- **Too much fire:** Melts everything at once. Resources slip away, creating waste or chaos.
- **Too much ice:** Holds too tightly, never allowing growth or expansion.
- **Balance:** When flame meets ice at the right pace, streams are released—measured, usable, and aligned with your goals.

This practice is about **timing and balance**: awakening what was locked, without destroying its structure.

Ritual of the Controlled Thaw

Purpose: To ignite opportunities that have been locked in stagnation, releasing them in a balanced way.

Materials Needed:

- A glass bowl with a large block of ice (frozen the night before)
- Three coins, frozen inside the ice (drop them in the water before freezing)
- A red candle (for flame)
- A small dish of cinnamon or cloves (to represent warmth and expansion)

Steps:

1. **Preparation of the Ice Block**
    - Place the bowl with the frozen block of ice before you. The coins within represent opportunities currently trapped.
2. **Lighting the Fire**
    - Light the red candle. Hold it above the ice (safe distance, do not let wax drip into the bowl).
    - Whisper: *"Flame awakens, but does not destroy. Melt with measure, wealth with joy."*
3. **Slow Thawing**
    - Move the candle flame in circles around the ice. Watch as droplets form and drip, gradually revealing the coins.
    - Sprinkle a pinch of cinnamon/cloves onto the ice as it melts, saying: *"Opportunity warms, riches flow steady."*
4. **Claiming the Released Wealth**
    - When one coin loosens, remove it carefully. Hold it in your hand and affirm: *"This gift arrives now, ready for me."*
    - Continue until all three coins are free, but resist rushing the process.

5.Closing the Ritual

- Snuff the candle, thanking both fire and ice for balance.
- Carry the coins in your wallet, purse, or money box as talismans of opportunities released.

Result: Within days, new opportunities begin appearing—job offers, collaborations, sudden sales, or unexpected inflows. They will come in manageable steps rather than overwhelming floods.

Three Opportunity Spells with Flame on Ice

1. The Candle-and-Ice Partnership

- Place a tealight on a saucer, and beside it, a small bowl of ice cubes.
- As the candle burns, the ice melts—representing opportunities being unlocked.
- Whisper: *"As flame softens frost, so fortune softens silence."*
- Pour the melted water over your front doorstep or threshold to welcome new chances into your home.

2. The Ember Coin Thaw

- Freeze a coin in a small cube of water.
- Place it on a fire-safe dish with a lit candle nearby.
- As the cube melts, recite: *"Bound no longer, flow returns."*
- Keep the coin in your wallet as a charm for opening blocked streams of income.

3. The Opportunity Key

- Take a metal key (real or symbolic) and freeze it overnight in a jar of water.
- The next day, light a candle and slowly thaw the jar beside it.
- As the key emerges, say: *"Ice yields, doors open, pathways align."*
- Carry the key as a charm to attract new ventures or to "unlock" hidden opportunities.

Meditation: The River Beneath the Ice

Purpose: To embody patience while trusting that abundance is already moving beneath the frozen surface.

1. Close your eyes and visualize a wide frozen river. Above it, snow lies heavy; beneath it, you sense water moving.
2. Imagine a candle flame in your hands. You lower it gently toward the surface—not to shatter, but to soften.
3. Watch as cracks form slowly, releasing a stream that begins to flow.
4. Whisper inwardly: *"I release what is ready. I hold what must wait."*
5. See yourself drinking from the flowing water, feeling it energize your body with fresh life.
6. Rest in the knowing: wealth flows beneath stillness, awaiting your signal to emerge.

Outcome: You emerge from meditation with the ability to discern timing—when to act, when to wait, and how to release opportunities at the right pace.

Chapter 6: The Final Melt — Unlocking Wealth Through Fire-Water Fusion

Every chapter until now has taught us to respect the wisdom of frost and the power of flame. Ice bound our debts, held our impulses, and preserved wealth. Fire ignited opportunity, thawed stagnation, and multiplied fortune in storm and spark. Yet these forces were always seen in tension—fire above, ice below; one pushing against the other.

The true secret of **Frostfire Prosperity** is not separation, but union. When flame and water join, they create steam—rising energy, invisible yet unstoppable. This is the essence of the **Final Melt**: a ritual of fusion, where ice and fire no longer struggle, but merge to birth something greater.

This chapter reveals how to use fire-water fusion as a final unlocking: releasing all hidden prosperity, dissolving scarcity, and elevating your wealth energy into its highest form.

The Alchemy of Fusion

- **Ice Alone:** Holds, protects, and preserves, but risks stagnation.
- **Fire Alone:** Expands, transforms, and accelerates, but risks destruction.
- **Together:** They create **flow and elevation**—abundance unlocked, moving upward as steam, impossible to contain.

Water carries wealth through channels. Fire carries willpower into action. When fused, they generate a current that multiplies opportunities, attracts gifts, and propels your fortune forward.

The Final Melt Ritual

Purpose: To release frozen wealth into flowing abundance, ignited by flame, guided into manifestation.

Materials:

- A clear glass bowl filled with ice cubes
- A red candle (for fire)
- A silver or white candle (for water/ice)
- Three coins (representing unlocked prosperity)
- A pinch of herbs for prosperity (cinnamon, basil, or bay leaf)

Steps:

1. **Setting the Stage**
    - Place the bowl of ice in the center of your altar or table. Tuck the three coins among the cubes.
    - Set the red candle to the right (fire) and the silver candle to the left (water/ice).
2. **Dual Ignition**
    - Light both candles, beginning with the silver. Say: *"By frost I preserve, by fire I release. Together, I am whole."*
3. **Merging the Forces**
    - Lift the red candle carefully and hold it close to the bowl. Watch as droplets begin to form on the ice.
    - Sprinkle the herbs gently over the melting cubes, saying: *"Herbs of wealth, rise in steam, carry my fortune to its dream."*
4. **Invocation of Fusion**
    - Alternate your gaze between the red flame and the melting ice. Speak:
      "No longer apart, fire and water,
      Fuse as steam, my wealth grows hotter.

Melt what binds, release the flow,
Fortune unlocked, now let it grow."

5. **Claiming the Coins**
   - As the coins loosen from the melting ice, remove them one by one.
   - With each coin, affirm a specific wealth goal (e.g., "This coin releases new income," "This coin releases financial freedom," "This coin releases wealth that lasts").
   - Dry and keep the coins as permanent prosperity talismans.
6. **Closing**
   - Let the candles burn for a few minutes more, then snuff them respectfully.
   - Pour the melted water outdoors at a crossroads or near the base of a tree, releasing the unlocked energy into the world.

Result: Opportunities, gifts, and wealth currents are no longer bound. Within weeks, unexpected openings appear—business growth, resources arriving just when needed, or financial relief emerging where there was once block.

Three Fusion Spells for Ongoing Abundance

1. Steam of Success

- Hold a cup of warm water over a candle flame.
- As steam rises, whisper: *"As vapor climbs, so rises my fortune."*
- Inhale gently, imagining yourself breathing in success.

2. The Boiling Pot of Opportunity

- Place a pot of water on the stove with three coins inside.
- Bring it to a gentle boil, chanting: *"Heat unlocks, fortune flows."*
- Remove coins with tongs, dry them, and keep them in your prosperity jar.

3. The Frostfire Drink

- Fill a glass with both ice cubes and hot water, letting them swirl together.
- As the ice cracks and hisses, say: *"From clash comes flow, from balance comes wealth."*
- Drink slowly, imagining the forces fusing within your body, charging you with abundance.

Meditation: Becoming the Flame-Water Union

Purpose: To integrate the lessons of frost and fire into your personal energy field.

1. Sit comfortably, eyes closed. Imagine yourself as a great frozen lake. Still, quiet, sealed.
2. Now see a golden flame descending, touching the surface. Instead of shattering, the ice begins to melt steadily.
3. Water flows beneath you, flame glows above you—and then both merge into rising steam.
4. See yourself dissolve into this mist, expanding upward, weightless and limitless. You are no longer frozen or burning—you are both, fused, eternal.
5. Whisper: *"I am frost. I am flame. I am the fortune that none can tame."*
6. Rest in the sensation of completeness, carrying this balance into your daily life.

Outcome: Your inner being holds the balance of preservation and expansion. Wealth flows not in extremes, but in harmony, rising continually like steam from fire-kissed water.

Closing Reflections

The journey of *Frostfire Fortune* has shown you how to freeze debt, ignite ambition, summon gifts, thrive in chaos, and unlock opportunities. Now, with the **Final Melt**, you stand at the union point—where no force is wasted, and every current of wealth becomes usable.

Ice and fire are no longer opposites within you. They are partners, fusing into a force that multiplies, rises, and carries you forward into prosperity. The season of frost is no longer a time of lack. It is your greatest ally.

From this day, you hold the secret of fire-water fusion: the power to **unlock wealth endlessly, no matter the season.**

Appendix A: Frostfire Ritual Toolkit

The rituals in this book are living practices, but they require the right tools to channel frost and flame effectively. The following **Frostfire Ritual Toolkit** is designed as your portable altar—objects and materials that you can assemble, consecrate, and keep ready for wealth work throughout the winter season (and beyond). Each tool represents a bridge between ice and fire, stillness and motion, preservation and expansion.

1. Core Frostfire Elements

a. Ice or Frozen Water

- Symbolism: Stillness, suspension, preservation, clarity.
- Uses: Freezing debt, holding impulses, mirroring reflection rituals.
- Pro Tip: Use filtered water for freezing, as clarity in ice enhances energetic purity.

b. Candle Flame

- Symbolism: Ambition, ignition, transformation, controlled thawing.
- Uses: Lighting opportunities, melting stagnation, multiplying fortune.
- Pro Tip: Red candles activate will and drive; white or silver candles stabilize and purify.

c. Steam or Vapor

- Symbolism: Fusion, release, rising energy, invisible wealth currents.
- Uses: Final Melt rituals, breathwork, prosperity meditations.
- Pro Tip: Pour boiling water into a heat-safe bowl during ritual and watch steam rise as a visualization of wealth's ascent.

2. Prosperity Carriers

a. Coins (Silver, Copper, or Gold)

- Represent tangible wealth and are used as “anchors” in ice or fire-water fusion.
- Freeze coins in water to symbolize trapped wealth being unlocked.
- Carry released coins as prosperity talismans in your wallet.

b. Herbs and Spices

- **Cinnamon**: Ignites prosperity quickly, accelerates income streams.
- **Cloves**: Adds warmth, stability, and protection against financial loss.
- **Bay Leaf**: Write wishes on leaves, then burn or freeze them to seal intent.
- **Basil**: Draws steady, household-centered prosperity.

c. Salt or Sugar

- White powders mimic snow, used in snowstorm spells or for dissolving debts.
- Creates a cleansing layer to obscure harmful influences.

3. Reflective Surfaces

a. Frozen Bowls of Water

- Essential for reflection rituals (Chapter 3).
- Can be placed under candles to combine mirror and flame.

b. Mirrors or Shiny Metal Surfaces

- Used to amplify and "bounce back" prosperity intentions.
- Best paired with coins or written requests placed upon them.

4. Containers of Stillness

a. Glass Jars

- Function as ice jars to freeze debts or reckless habits.
- Represent sealed contracts between your will and the frost.

b. Small Bowls or Dishes

- Used for offerings, melting rituals, or holding snow-like powders.
- Choose glass or ceramic for clarity and resilience.

5. Ritual Accessories

a. Ribbons or Cloths (White, Silver, Red)

- White: Stillness, reflection, purity.
- Silver: Wealth echo, moonlight clarity.
- Red: Flame of action, passion, ignition of opportunity.
- Use to bind spells or create symbolic bridges between fire and frost.

b. Keys

- Represent unlocking opportunities once frozen.
- Freeze a key in water and thaw with candle flame to symbolize doorways opening.

c. Magnets

- Used in snowdrift-gathering spells to draw scattered wealth back into unity.
- Keep near financial records or money jars as a constant pull for abundance.

6. Supportive Tools

a. Writing Implements & Paper

- For recording debts, writing requests, and sealing intentions into jars or ice.
- Blue or black ink for grounding, gold or silver ink for expansion.

b. Altar Cloth

- Preferably in deep blue, silver, or white. Provides a sacred surface for laying out your toolkit.
- Protects surfaces during melting or burning rituals.

c. Small Offering Dishes

- For gifts of herbs, coins, or water to the unseen currents of prosperity.

7. Daily Use Practices

To make the toolkit more than ceremonial, integrate it into daily life:

- **Morning Candle:** Light a small candle over a single ice cube to remind yourself of balance—discipline and passion together.
- **Wallet Coin:** Always carry one coin that has been frozen and thawed in ritual, as a charm of released opportunity.
- **Threshold Sprinkle:** Pour melted ritual water across your front step once a week to invite prosperity into your home.
- **Weekly Offering:** Place a coin or bay leaf on your frozen bowl, leaving it overnight, then dispose of it outdoors as a gift to the currents that support your wealth.

8. Consecration of the Toolkit

Before using your tools, bring them together in one ritual:

1. Place ice at the center of your altar, surrounded by candles.
2. Arrange coins, herbs, mirrors, jars, and accessories around it.
3. Light the candles, saying:
   "By frost I preserve, by flame I release. These tools now serve wealth and peace."
4. Sprinkle a few drops of melted ice water on each item to consecrate them in frostfire balance.

Final Note

The Frostfire Ritual Toolkit is more than objects—it is a mindset container. Each piece reminds you that abundance requires both stillness and ignition. Keep your toolkit accessible, cared for, and refreshed with seasonal adjustments. Over time, these tools will carry your energy, amplifying each ritual's effect and building a resonance field where prosperity feels natural, constant, and unstoppable.

Appendix B: Seasonal Prosperity Calendar

Prosperity flows not only through rituals but through rhythm. Nature teaches us that abundance is seasonal: winter preserves, spring awakens, summer expands, autumn gathers. By aligning your frostfire practice with these cycles, you transform ritual into lifestyle.

This **Seasonal Prosperity Calendar** offers a framework of practices for each season, ensuring that wealth energy is cultivated, preserved, expanded, and harvested year-round.

Winter (December – February): The Season of Preservation
Theme: Freeze, reflect, and stabilize.

- **Monthly Focus:**
    - December: Pause and seal financial leaks.
    - January: Build clarity through ice jar rituals.
    - February: Practice reflection offerings to prepare for spring growth.

Core Practices:

- **Weekly Ice Jar Freezing:** Write down debts, fears, or reckless habits and freeze them. Replace old slips weekly.
- **Mirror Bowl Offering:** Place coins on frozen water once a month, asking for multiplied return.
- **Meditation:** Visualize your wealth as a frozen lake—calm, still, protected. Whisper: *"Preserved, not lost."*

Seasonal Ritual:
On the Winter Solstice, freeze three coins in ice. At midnight, place them in candlelight, reciting: *"In the longest night, fortune is sealed for light."* Keep them until spring thaw.

Spring (March – May): The Season of Awakening
Theme: Thaw, ignite, and open.

- **Monthly Focus:**
    - March: Controlled thawing (release frozen wealth).
    - April: Ignite new ventures with flame-on-ice rituals.
    - May: Plant prosperity seeds for future harvest.

Core Practices:

- **Thawing Rituals:** Freeze coins or keys, then melt them with candle flame to symbolize opportunities opening.
- **Seed Blessings:** Bury bay leaves or coins in soil to "sprout" financial growth.
- **Meditation:** Imagine yourself thawing from winter, warmed by golden light. Say: *"I awaken wealth with balance."*

Seasonal Ritual:

At the Spring Equinox, place a bowl of melting ice under the sun. As water drips, scatter basil leaves, chanting: *"As frost gives way, my fortune grows."*

Summer (June – August): The Season of Expansion
Theme: Burn bright, multiply, and manifest.

- **Monthly Focus:**
  - June: Ignite projects with summer flame rituals.
  - July: Call storms to multiply fortune (snowstorm spellcasting adapted as "firestorm summoning").
  - August: Anchor expansion with grounding rituals.

Core Practices:

- **Candle-on-Ice Rituals:** Use tealights above frozen bowls, symbolizing fire fueling flow.
- **Opportunity Keys:** Carry a key thawed in ritual to unlock doors of growth.
- **Meditation:** Visualize yourself as a flame rising, unafraid of vastness. Say: *"I expand wealth without fear."*

Seasonal Ritual:

On the Summer Solstice, place three candles around a frozen bowl. As it melts in the heat, chant: *"Fire and frost, joined in might, expand my fortune in the light."* Pour melted water on your doorstep.

Autumn (September – November): The Season of Harvest
Theme: Gather, balance, and prepare for preservation.

- **Monthly Focus:**
    - September: Reflect on gains and call back scattered wealth.
    - October: Use storm rituals to multiply final streams of abundance.
    - November: Seal what is gathered for winter preservation.

Core Practices:

- **Snowdrift Gathering Rituals:** Use magnets, rice, or sugar to symbolically gather scattered finances into one pile.
- **Debt Dissolver:** Cover written debts with salt or sugar to obscure their influence.
- **Meditation:** Imagine a harvest field glowing with plenty. Say: *"I gather all that is mine, safely stored."*

Seasonal Ritual:

At the Autumn Equinox, lay out coins in a circle on a white cloth. Sprinkle them with cinnamon while saying: *"As leaves fall, wealth is gathered."* Collect coins and store them in your prosperity jar.

Daily & Weekly Prosperity Rhythm

Regardless of season, these simple habits keep frostfire energy active:

- **Daily:** Light a candle over an ice cube in the morning for balance. Whisper your intent for the day.
- **Weekly:** Pour melted ritual water at your threshold to welcome prosperity.
- **Monthly:** Perform one major ritual aligned with the seasonal focus.

Closing Note: Living in Seasons of Wealth

This calendar reminds us that prosperity is not a single event but a **cycle**. Winter preserves, spring awakens, summer expands, autumn gathers. The Frostfire Path teaches us to honor each stage, knowing that wealth is always moving—sometimes hidden, sometimes rising, always present.

By living with this rhythm, you not only practice magick but embody prosperity as a natural state of being.

Appendix C: Frostfire Journal Prompts

Wealth magick is more than ritual—it is awareness. Each spell, meditation, and seasonal practice in this book unlocks opportunities, but it is journaling that reveals the deeper patterns of how prosperity flows in your life. Writing is itself a ritual: your pen becomes a flame, your page the frozen lake, and each word an offering that reflects back to you multiplied.

The following prompts are organized into three groups—**Ice Prompts, Fire Prompts, and Fusion Prompts**—to mirror the core frostfire cycle. They may be used daily, weekly, or seasonally. Write slowly, honestly, and with focus. Revisit entries often to see where hidden wealth is preserved, where it is thawing, and where it is ready to rise.

I. Ice Prompts: Preserving, Freezing, and Clarifying

Use these prompts when you need to stabilize finances, pause reckless impulses, or reflect with clarity.

1. What current debts, habits, or worries feel like they are "draining heat" from my life?
2. If I could freeze one recurring financial pattern for 30 days, what would it be?
3. Which areas of my life feel still, but not dead—waiting beneath the ice for the right time?
4. What do I want preserved from this season (resources, ideas, savings) to be carried into the next?
5. What emotional "noise" do I need to place into an ice jar so that I can think clearly about wealth?
6. How does winter stillness sharpen my vision instead of limiting it?
7. Where am I mistaking pause for failure?

II. Fire Prompts: Igniting, Expanding, and Acting

Use these prompts when energy feels stagnant, when opportunity appears, or when you need to call movement into your financial life.

1. What am I ready to thaw and release into flow this week?
2. If flame is my willpower, where must I direct it most urgently?
3. What opportunities are glowing faintly in my life, waiting to be fanned into full fire?
4. Where have I burned too hot—too quickly—and what did that teach me about pacing?
5. If I could ignite one bold financial action without fear, what would it be?
6. How can I transform a recent challenge into fuel for prosperity?
7. What wealth or resources already present in my life deserve recognition and gratitude?

III. Fusion Prompts: Balance, Steam, and the Final Melt

Use these prompts when you want to embody balance, integrate lessons, or elevate prosperity into long-term flow.

1. Where in my life do I need more ice (restraint, patience)? Where do I need more fire (action, risk)?
2. How can I ensure my wealth grows at a sustainable pace instead of flooding or freezing?
3. What would it look like if I held stillness and ambition equally in my decisions?
4. When flame meets ice in me, what steam rises—what invisible energy carries me forward?
5. How do I know when the time is right to release preserved wealth into action?
6. If I am both frost and fire, what kind of prosperity is uniquely mine to manifest?
7. What long-term legacy do I want my Frostfire practice to create in my life and for others?

Seasonal Journal Cycle

To integrate prompts into your **Seasonal Prosperity Calendar** (Appendix B):

- **Winter:** Use Ice Prompts weekly to track what you are preserving and freezing.
- **Spring:** Use Fire Prompts to set intentions for thawing and growth.
- **Summer:** Blend Fire and Fusion Prompts to maximize expansion.
- **Autumn:** Use Ice and Fusion Prompts to record what you gather, store, and prepare for the next cycle.

Closing Practice

Before each journaling session, place a single **ice cube** in a small dish and a **candle** beside it. Light the candle, then begin writing. As the cube slowly melts, let it symbolize your frozen thoughts turning fluid on the page. When you finish, pour the melted water at your threshold or near a plant, releasing your reflections into the world as living energy.

◈ With these Frostfire Journal Prompts, writing becomes part of your wealth magick. Each entry is a crack in the ice, each reflection a spark of flame. Over time, your journal becomes a mirror of your prosperity journey—a frozen lake and burning torch bound together, always reflecting, always igniting.

Message from the Author:

I hope you enjoyed this book, I love astrology and knew there was not a book such as this out on the shelf. I love metaphysical items as well. Please check out my other books:

-Life of Government Benefits

-My life of Hell

-My life with Hydrocephalus

-Red Sky

-World Domination:Woman's rule

-World Domination:Woman's Rule 2: The War

-Life and Banishment of Apophis: book 1

-The Kidney Friendly Diet

-The Ultimate Hemp Cookbook

-Creating a Dispensary(legally)

-Cleanliness throughout life: the importance of showering from childhood to adulthood.

-Strong Roots: The Risks of Overcoddling children

-Hemp Horoscopes: Cosmic Insights and Earthly Healing

- Celestial Hemp Navigating the Zodiac: Through the Green Cosmos

-Astrological Hemp: Aligning The Stars with Earth's Ancient Herb

-The Astrological Guide to Hemp: Stars, Signs, and Sacred Leaves

-Green Growth: Innovative Marketing Strategies for your Hemp Products and Dispensary

-Cosmic Cannabis

-Astrological Munchies

-Henry The Hemp

-Zodiacal Roots: The Astrological Soul Of Hemp

- **Green Constellations: Intersection of Hemp and Zodiac**

-Hemp in The Houses: An astrological Adventure Through The Cannabis Galaxy

-Galactic Ganja Guide

Heavenly Hemp

Zodiac Leaves

Doctor Who Astrology

Cannastrology

Stellar Satvias and Cosmic Indicas

Celestial Cannabis: A Zodiac Journey

AstroHerbology: The Sky and The Soil: Volume 1

AstroHerbology:Celestial Cannabis:Volume 2

Cosmic Cannabis Cultivation

The Starry Guide to Herbal Harmony: Volume 1

The Starry Guide to Herbal Harmony: Cannabis Universe: Volume 2

Yugioh Astrology: Astrological Guide to Deck, Duels and more

Nightmare Mansion: Echoes of The Abyss

Nightmare Mansion 2: Legacy of Shadows

Nightmare Mansion 3: Shadows of the Forgotten

Nightmare Mansion 4: Echoes of the Damned

The Life and Banishment of Apophis: Book 2

Nightmare Mansion: Halls of Despair

Healing with Herb: Cannabis and Hydrocephalus

Planetary Pot: Aligning with Astrological Herbs: Volume 1

Fast Track to Freedom: 30 Days to Financial Independence Using AI, Assets, and Agile Hustles

Cosmic Hemp Pathways

How to Become Financially Free in 30 Days: 10,000 Paths to Prosperity

Zodiacal Herbage: Astrological Insights: Volume 1

Nightmare Mansion: Whispers in the Walls

The Daleks Invade Atlantis

Henry the hemp and Hydrocephalus

10X The Kidney Friendly Diet

Cannabis Universe: Adult coloring book

Hemp Astrology: The Healing Power of the Stars

Zodiacal Herbage: Astrological Insights: Cannabis Universe: Volume 2

Planetary Pot: Aligning with Astrological Herbs: Cannabis Universes: Volume 2

Doctor Who: Convergence Protocol – The Replicator War

Nightmare Mansion: Curse of the Blood Moon

The Celestial Stoner: A Guide to the Zodiac

Cosmic Pleasures: Sex Toy Astrology for Every Sign

Hydrocephalus Astrology: Navigating the Stars and Healing Waters

Lapis and the Mischievous Chocolate Bar

Celestial Positions: Sexual Astrology for Every Sign

Apophis's Shadow Work Journal: **:** A Journey of Self-Discovery and Healing

Kinky Cosmos: Sexual Kink Astrology for Every Sign

Digital Cosmos: The Astrological Digimon Compendium

Stellar Seeds: The Cosmic Guide to Growing with Astrology

Apophis's Daily Gratitude Journal

Cat Astrology: Feline Mysteries of the Cosmos

The Cosmic Kama Sutra: An Astrological Guide to Sexual Positions

Unleash Your Potential: A Guided Journal Powered by AI Insights

Whispers of the Enchanted Grove

Cosmic Pleasures: An Astrological Guide to Sexual Kinks

369, 12 Manifestation Journal

Whisper of the nocturne journal(blank journal for writing or drawing)

The Boogey Book

Locked In Reflection: A Chastity Journey Through Locktober

Generating Wealth Quickly:How to Generate $100,000 in 24 Hours

Star Magic: Harness the Power of the Universe

The Flatulence Chronicles: A Fart Journal for Self-Discovery

The Doctor and The Death Moth

Seize the Day: A Personal Seizure Tracking Journal

The Ultimate Boogeyman Safari: A Journey into the Boogie World and Beyond

Whispers of Samhain: 1,000 Spells of Love, Luck, and Lunar Magic: Samhain Spell Book

Apophis's guides:Witch's Spellbook Crafting Guide for Halloween

Frost & Flame: The Enchanted Yule Grimoire of 1000 Winter Spells

The Ultimate Boogey Goo Guide & Spooky Activities for Halloween Fun

Harmony of the Scales: A Libra's Spellcraft for Balance and Beauty

The Enchanted Advent: 36 Days of Christmas Wonders

Nightmare Mansion: The Labyrinth of Screams

Harvest of Enchantment: 1,000 Spells of Gratitude, Love, and Fortune for Thanksgiving

The Boogey Chronicles: A Journal of Nightly Encounters and Shadowy Secrets

The 12 Days of Financial Freedom: A Step-by-Step Christmas Countdown to Transform Your Finances

Sigil of the Eternal Spiral Blank Journal

A Christmas Feast: Timeless Recipes for Every Meal

Holiday Stress-Free Solutions: A Survival Guide to Thriving During the Festive Season

Yu-Gi-Oh! Holiday Gifting Mastery: The Ultimate Guide for Fans and Newcomers Alike

Holiday Harmony: A Hydrocephalus Survival Guide for the Festive Season

Celestial Craft: The Witch's Almanac for 2025 – A Cosmic Guide to Manifestations, Moons, and Mystical Events

Doctor Who: The Toymaker's Winter Wonderland

Tulsa King Unveiled: A Thrilling Guide to Stallone's Mafia Masterpiece

Pendulum Craft: A Complete Guide to Crafting and Using Personalized Divination Tools

Nightmare Mansion: Santa's Eternal Eve

Starlight Noel: A Cosmic Journey through Christmas Mysteries

The Dark Architect: Unlocking the Blueprint of Existence

Surviving the Embrace: The Ultimate Guide to Encounters with The Hugging Molly

The Enchanted Codex: Secrets of the Craft for Witches, Wiccans, and Pagans

Harvest of Gratitude: A Complete Thanksgiving Guide

Yuletide Essentials: A Complete Guide to an Authentic and Magical Christmas

Celestial Smokes: A Cosmic Guide to Cigars and Astrology

Living in Balance: A Comprehensive Survival Guide to Thriving with Diabetes Insipidus

Cosmic Symbiosis: The Venom Zodiac Chronicles

The Cursed Paw of Ambition

Cosmic Symbiosis: The Astrological Venom Journal

Celestial Wonders Unfold: A Stargazer's Guide to the Cosmos (2024-2029)

The Ultimate Black Friday Prepper's Guide: Mastering Shopping Strategies and Savings

Cosmic Sales: The Astrological Guide to Black Friday Shopping

Legends of the Corn Mother and Other Harvest Myths

Whispers of the Harvest: The Corn Mother's Journal

The Evergreen Spellbook

The Doctor Meets the Boogeyman

The White Witch of Rose Hall's SpellBook

The Gingerbread Golem's Shadow: A Study in Sweet Darkness

The Gingerbread Golem Codex: An Academic Exploration of Sweet Myths

The Gingerbread Golem Grimoire: Sweet Magicks and Spells for the Festive Witch

The Curse of the Gingerbread Golem

10-minute Christmas Crafts for kids

Christmas Crisis Solutions: The Ultimate Last-Minute Survival Guide

Gingerbread Golem Recipes: Holiday Treats with a Magical Twist

The Infinite Key: Unlocking Mystical Secrets of the Ages

Enchanted Yule: A Wiccan and Pagan Guide to a Magical and Memorable Season

Dinosaurs of Power: Unlocking Ancient Magick

Astro-Dinos: The Cosmic Guide to Prehistoric Wisdom

Gallifrey's Yule Logs: A Festive Doctor Who Cookbook

The Dino Grimoire: Secrets of Prehistoric Magick

The Gift They Never Knew They Needed

The Gingerbread Golem's Culinary Alchemy: Enchanting Recipes for a Sweetly Dark Feast

A Time Lord Christmas: Holiday Adventures with the Doctor

Krampusproofing Your Home: Defensive Strategies for Yule

Silent Frights: A Collection of Christmas Creepypastas to Chill Your Bones

Santa Raptor's Jolly Carnage: A Dino-Claus Christmas Tale

Prehistoric Palettes: A Dino Wicca Coloring Journey

The Christmas Wishkeeper Chronicles

The Starlight Sleigh: A Holiday Journey

Elf Secrets: The True Magic of the North Pole

Candy Cane Conjurations

Cooking with Kids: Recipes Under 20 Minutes

Doctor Who: The TARDIS Confiscation

The Anxiety First Aid Kit: Quick Tools to Calm Your Mind

Frosty Whispers: A Winter's Tale

The Infinite Key: Unlocking the Secrets to Prosperity, Resilience, and Purpose

The Grasping Void: Why You'll Regret This Purchase

Astrology for Busy Bees: Star Signs Simplified

The Instant Focus Formula: Cut Through the Noise

The Secret Language of Colors: Unlocking the Emotional Codes

Sacred Fossil Chronicles: Blank Journal

The Christmas Cottage Miracle

Feeding Frenzy: Graboid-Inspired Recipes

Manifest in Minutes: The Quick Law of Attraction Guide

The Symbiote Chronicles: Doctor Who's Venomous Journey

Think Tiny, Grow Big: The Minimalist Mindset

The Energy Key: Unlocking Limitless Motivation

New Year, New Magic: Manifesting Your Best Year Yet

Unstoppable You: Mastering Confidence in Minutes

Infinite Energy: The Secret to Never Feeling Drained

Lightning Focus: Mastering the Art of Productivity in a Distracted World

Saturnalia Manifestation Magick: A Guide to Unlocking Abundance During the Solstice

Graboids and Garland: The Ultimate Tremors-Themed Christmas Guide

12 Nights of Holiday Magic

The Power of Pause: 60-Second Mindfulness Practices

The Quick Reset: How to Reclaim Your Life After Burnout

The Shadow Eater: A Tale of Despair and Survival

The Micro-Mastery Method: Transform Your Skills in Just Minutes a Day

Reclaiming Time: How to Live More by Doing Less

Chronovore: The Eternal Nexus

The Mind Reset: Unlocking Your Inner Peace in a Chaotic World

Confidence Code: Building Unshakable Self-Belief

Baby the Vampire Terrier
Baby the Vampire Terrier's Christmas Adventure
Celestial Streams: The Content Creator's Astrology Manual
The Wealth Whisperer: Unlocking Abundance with Everyday Actions
The Energy Equation: Maximize Your Output Without Burning Out
The Happiness Algorithm: Science-Backed Steps to Joyful Living
Stress-Free Success: Achieving Goals Without Anxiety
Mindful Wealth: The New Blueprint for Financial Freedom
The Festive Flavors of New Year: A Culinary Celebration
The Master's Gambit: Keys of Eternal Power
Shadowed Secrets: Groundhog Day Mysteries
Beneath the Burrow: Lessons from the Groundhog
Spring's Whispers: The Groundhog's Prediction
The Limitless Mindset: Unlock Your Untapped Potential
The Focus Funnel: How to Cut Through Chaos and Get Results
Bold Moves: Building Courage to Live on Your Terms
The Daily Shift: Simple Practices for Lasting Transformation
The Quarter-Life Reset: Thriving in Your 20s and 30s
The Art of Shadowplay: Building Your Own Personal Myth
The Eternal Loop: Finding Purpose in Repetition
Burrowing Wisdom: Life Lessons from the Groundhog
Shadow Work: A Groundhog Day Perspective
Love in Bloom: 5-Minute Romantic Gestures
The Shadowspell Codex: Secrets of Forbidden Magick
The Burnout Cure: Finding Balance in a Busy World
The Groundhog Prophecy: Unlocking Seasonal Secrets
Nog Tales: The Spirited History of Eggnog
Six More Weeks: Embracing Seasonal Transitions
The Lumivian Chronicles: Fragments of the Fifth Dimension
Money on Your Mind: A Beginner's Guide to Wealth
The Focus Fix: Breaking Through Distraction

January's Spirit Keepers: Mystical Protectors of the Cold
Creativity Unchained: Unlocking Your Wildest Ideas in 2025
Manifestation Mastery: 365 Days to Rewrite Your Reality
The Groundhog's Mirror: Reflecting on Change
The Weeping Angels' Christmas Curse
Burrowed in Time: A Groundhog Day Journey
Heartbeats: Poems to Share with Your Valentine
Dino Wicca: The Sacred Grimoire of Prehistoric Magick
Courage of the Pride: Finding Your Inner Roar
The Lion's Leap: Bold Moves for Big Results
Healthy Hustle: Achieving Without Overworking
Practical Manifesting: Turning Dreams into Reality in 2025
Jurassic Pharaohs: Unlocking the Magick of Ancient Egypt and Dino Wicca
The Happiness Equation: Small Changes for Big Joy
The Confidence Compass: Finding Your Inner Strength
Whispers in the Hollow: Tales of the Forgotten Beasts
Echoes from the Hollow: The Return of Forgotten Beasts
The Hollow Ascendant: The Rise of the Forgotten Beasts
The Relationship Reset: Building Better Connections
Mastering the Morning: How to Win the Day Before 8 AM
The Shadow's Dance: Groundhog Day Symbolism
Cupid's Kitchen: Quick Valentine's Day Recipes
Valentine's Day on a Budget: Love Without Breaking the Bank
Astrocraft: Aligning the Stars in the World of Minecraft
Forecasting Life: Groundhog Day Reflections

Bleeding Hearts: Twisted Tales of Valentine's Terror

Herbal Smoke Revolution: The Ultimate Guide to Nature's Cigarette Alternative

Winter's Wrath: The Complete Survival Blueprint for Extreme Freezes.

The Groundhog's Shadow: A Tale of Seasons
Burrowed Insights: Wisdom from the Groundhog

Sensual Strings: The Art of Erotic Bondage

Whispered Flames: Unlocking the Power of Fire Play

Forgotten Shadows: A Guide to Cryptids Lost to Time

Six Weeks of Secrets: Groundhog Day's Hidden Messages

Shadows and Cycles: Groundhog Day Reflections

The Art of Love Letters: Crafting the Perfect Message

Romantic Getaways at Home: Turning Your Space into Paradise

Purrfect Brews: A Cat Lover's Guide to Coffee and Companionship

The Groundhog's Wisdom: Timeless Lessons for Modern Life

The Shadow Oracle: Groundhog Day as a Predictor

Emerging from the Burrow: A Journey of Renewal

The Language of Love: Learning Your Partner's Love Style

Authorpreneur: The Ultimate Blueprint for Writing, Publishing, and Thriving as an Author

Weathering the Seasons: Groundhog Day Perspectives

Valentine's Day Magic: A Guide to Romantic Rituals

The Shadow Chronicles: Stories of Groundhog Day

Love and Laughter: Fun Games for Valentine's Day

AstroRealty: Unlocking the Stars for Property Success

The Groundhog's Path: A Guide to Seasonal Balance

Groundhog Day Diaries: Reflections in the Shadow

The Groundhog's Light: Illuminating the Path Ahead

Valentine's Traditions from Around the World

AI Wealth Revolution: Unlocking the Trillionaire Mindset

Love Rekindled: Reigniting Passion in Relationships

Single and Thriving: Self-Love on Valentine's Day

Emerald Legends: Mystical Tales of Ireland

Green Alchemy: Harnessing Nature's Magic

The Hearts of Horror: A Valentine's Day Nightmare

The Leprechaun's Guide to Wealth and Wisdom

Dancing with the Sidhe: Celebrating the Otherworld

Shamrocks and Shadows: Mysteries of the Green Isle
Emerald Energy: Harnessing Luck and Growth
The Gingerbread Golem's Valentine: A Sweetheart's Guide to Love and Enchantment
The Celtic Knot: Weaving Life and Destiny
Green Fire: Elemental Magic for St. Patrick's Day
Clover Chronicles: Finding Your Inner Luck
Ireland's Mystical Creatures: A Field Guide
Gingerbread Golem's Love Almanac
Prowl and Thrive: The Lion's Guide to Success
Love Alchemy: Transforming Your Life Through Heart Energy
WORLD DOMINATION: Woman's Rule 3:The New Life
The Midnight Rose: A Guide to Lunar Love Spells
The Forbidden Letters: Writing Your Own Love Prophecy
Luck and Lore: St. Patrick's Day for Modern Mystics
The Green Path: A Pagan Celebration of Renewal
The Dark Architect's Guide to Reprogramming Reality
Prankster's Paradise: A Guide to Harmless Hijinks
Manifest Your Reality: The Law of Attraction Simplified
The TARDIS Owner's Manual: Understanding the Doctor's Ship: *A complete guide to the TARDIS, its technology, secrets, and mysteries*
Starlit Romance: Astrology Secrets for Finding True Love
The Time Lord's Atlas: A Complete Guide to the Whoniverse: ***A breakdown of the locations, planets, and dimensions explored in Doctor Who***
Sweetheart Shadows: The Dark Side of Love and Attraction
February Fire: Reigniting Passion in Every Area of Life
The Self-Love Toolkit: 5 Ways to Embrace Who You Are
February Sparks: Ignite Your Dreams in 28 Days
March to Success: A 31-Day Action Blueprint
Ancient Paths: The 13 Sacred Principles of Dino Wicca

Echoes of Tomorrow: Navigating the AI Revolution
The Wellness Blueprint: Balancing Mind, Body, and Soul
Green Horizons: Sustainable Living for a Better Tomorrow
The AI Wealth Code: How to Make Millions with Automation
AI-Powered Creativity: Writing, Art, and Music for Profit
Extinction Rites: Rebirthing Your Soul Through Prehistoric Magick
Sacred Serpents tarot
Celestial Enchantment blank journal
Star Strains
Culinary Journeys: Exploring Global Flavors at Home
The Hollowvale Curse
The Hollowvale Harvest
The Egg of Transformation: Awakening Your Inner Power
Blooming Into Power: A Wiccan Guide to Spring Awakening
The Nightmare Nexus: The Third Doctor's Perilous Haunting
Digital Detox: Reclaiming Your Life in a Connected World
Ostara's Path: Walking the Spiral of Renewal
The Sacred Hare
Financial Freedom: Building Wealth in the Modern Age
Spring's Cauldron: Stirring the Waters of Change
The Hollowvale Pact
Quantum Consciousness: The Science of Reality Shifting
The Hollowvale Hunger
The Sacred Waters Within: A Witch's Guide to Hydrocephalus Magick
The Raven's Nest: Building a Life of Unshakable Stability
AI and the Human Mind: The Future of Intelligence
The Hollowvale Reckoning
Timeless Love: Building and Maintaining Lasting Relationships
The Raven's Roar: Unlocking Unstoppable Confidence
Raven Sight: Awakening Intuition and Inner Wisdom

The Butterfly Effect: Small Changes, Big Transformations
Taming the Boogeyman: How to Conquer Your Inner Fears
The Magick of Green: Awakening Earth's Energy in You
The Entrepreneurial Mindset: Secrets to Business Success
The Hollowvale End
The Shadow Luck Ritual: Reclaiming Power from Your Dark Side
Spring Magick for Beginners: A Simple Guide to Seasonal Energy Work
Doctor Who: The Hollowvale Conundrum
The March of Miracles: Unlocking Synchronicities in Spring
Unveiling the Cosmos: A Guide to Stargazing and Space Exploration
The Ultimate Guide to Surviving an Economic Collapse
The AI Gold Rush: How to Profit from the AI Revolution
Bastet's Shadow: The Hidden Power of Feline Magick
The Bastet Codex: Unlocking the Goddess's Magickal Secrets
Purring Spells: Harnessing Bastet's Healing Frequencies
Bastet's Nine Lives: Rebirth, Transformation, and Immortality Spells
Primal Currents: Hydrocephalus Magick in the Path of Dino Wicca
The Digital Gold Rush: Mastering E-Commerce and Online Sales
Future Shock: Adapting to the Next Decade of Change
The Quantum Mindset: Think Like a Billionaire
Sacred Motherhood: Awakening the Divine Feminine Within
The Mother's Spellbook: Enchantments for Love, Protection, and Prosperity
The Witch's Guide to Parenting: Raising Empowered and Intuitive Children
The Magick of Motherhood: Reclaiming Your Power Through Rituals

The Pagan Path to Self-Love: A Goddess's Guide to Worth and Confidence
Wild Woman Magick: Unleashing Your Primal Power
The Money Magnet Blueprint: Unlocking Unlimited Wealth
Biohacking 101: Unlock Your Body's Full Potential
The Wild Father: A Pagan Guide to Strength and Wisdom
The Sacred Masculine: Unlocking Your Inner Power
The Druid's Compass
The Warrior's Mindset
The Father's Fire
Odin's Path
Ancestral Bonds
The House That Whispers
The Magician's Code
The Wild Hunt
The Green Man's Path
The Altar of Success
The Shadow and the Sword
The High Priestess's Guide to Energy Healing
The Lunar Mother
The Sacred Self-Care Grimoire
The Womb Wisdom Codex
The Wheel of the Mother
The Witch's Guide to Manifestation
The Q2 Reset
The Ultimate Guide to AI-Powered Passive Income
Escape the 9-5
AI Feline Fortunes
The Tear-Stained Grimoire
Razorblade Runes
Cemetery Sirens
The Midnight Wristwatch
The Town That Forgets

AI Horror & Creepypasta
The Hollow Frequency
The Breach Echo
The Quiet Between Worlds
The Sigil of Tharan-Khul
Summon the Vault of Y'ha'ten
The Becoming Codex
The Profit of Az'ra-nar
The Drowned Logos
Echoes of the Eldritch Will
The Deep Ledger
Necronomicon of Networth
Covenant of the Wealthwyrm
The Whisperer's Manifesto
The Rites of Azh-K'luth
The Ark of the Crawling Coin
The Tithe of Shadows
Inkheart Abyss
The Timewinds of Y'ha-nthlei
The Spiral Labyrinth of Azag-Nirrh
The Gallifreyan Heresy of the Black Pharaoh
The Psalms of Nyog-Sotha
Black Rain Alchemy
The Infinite Maw
The Entropic Blueprint
The Oracle of Sh'guul
The Book of Breach
The Drowned Saint's Testament
Dreamcraft of the Sleeper God
The Silence Market
Cthonomics: The Dark Wealth Algorithm
Invocation of the Ten-Eyed King
Wealthbound to the Wyrm Below

Become the Unnameable
Codex of the Sovereign Flame
Rituals of Relentless Becoming
The Shadow Ascends
The Eyes Beneath You
The Will That Wakes Worlds
Silence Is a Weapon
The Mirror That Screams
The Whisper Between Moments
The Mind That Devours Fear
The Myth of the Finished Self
The Architect of Your Madness
The Voice You've Buried
The Discipline of Madness
Stormborn: Awakening Your Inner Tempest
The Mind That Ate Time
Unbind Your Becoming
The Pact You Owe Yourself
The Devourer's Diet
The Acid That Carves the Path
The Tower You Must Burn
The Breath Between Worlds
Speak Like the Deep
The Labyrinth Within
The Spine of the Sea God
Rejection Is a Portal
The Crown You Refused
The Scar Is the Spell
The Lightless Flame
The Habit of Becoming Horrific
ChickenJockey Chaos
The Gatekeeper Within
You Are Not Your Name

The Compass of the Mad
The Archive of Unsent Letters
What the Mirror Can't Show You
The Knife You Needed
Worship Nothing, Become Everything
The Other Voice
The Body the World Forgot
The Vein of the Void
The Black Bone Codex
The Puzzle of the Hidden Self (Millennium Puzzle)
The Eye That Sees the Lie *(Millennium Eye)*
The Ring of Return (Millennium Ring)
The Rod of Relentless Will ***(Millennium Rod)***
The Tally of the Soul (Millennium Tauk/Necklace)
The Key to the Locked Timeline (Millennium Key)
The Scale of Sacred Decisions (Millennium Scales)
Inferno Bites: The UnOfficial Minecraft Lava Cookbook
Rot in the Attic
Prana: The Hidden Force of Your Infinite Self
The Shadow Realm Within: Transforming Darkness Into Destiny
The Borderland Collapse
Claws of Protection: Bastet's Defensive Magick
Mr. Ring-a-Ding's Madness
Yugioh Astrology: Celestial Deckcraft and Duel Destiny (2026–2027 Edition)
The Seal You Signed: Unlocking the Power You Once Feared
The Puzzle of Infinite Minds: Unlocking the Mentalism Hidden Within
The Eye That Mirrors the All: Secrets of Inner Reflection
Doctor Who: The Toymaker's Broadcast
The Rod of Eternal Flow: Commanding the Currents of Vibration

Golden Eyes of Bastet: Enhancing Psychic Vision
The Key of Dual Forces: Balance Within the Polarity
The Scales of Living Rhythm: Timing the Dance of Life
The Necklace of Hidden Cause: Weaving the Webs of Fate
The Ring of Secret Masters: Rising Through the All Within All
Daggers of the Dying Deep
Bastet's Wealth and Fortune Magick: Prosperity Rituals of the Goddess
The Tide that Speaks
The Scrolls of Petosiris: 13 Rituals from the Feathered Eye
Petosiris and the Living Plague of Osirion
Feline Fire: Bastet's Passion and Love Magick
The Star Altar of Petosiris
Bastet's Whiskers: Supernatural Sensory Magick
The Bastet Grimoire
Feeding the Shadows
The Mouthless Prayer
The Spiral Wound
Becoming the Ibis: Lessons from Petosiris's Mind
The Crimson Coven: Cola Magick for Sweet Dominion
Sacred Cat's Paw
The Soda Zodiac: A Flavor for Every Sign
Covenant of the Crawling Flame
The Ink of Ish'Zur
Frothroot: The Thirst That Ate the World
The Golden Glyphs of Prosperity
The Etherbind Codex
Echoes of the Resistance: Reclaiming the You That Survived
Harnessed Minds: Breaking Free from Mental Control
The Eyes in the Smoke
Rootwake: The Carbon Covenant
Skitter Logic: Unlearning the Fear That Built You

Doctor Who: The World That Froths
Rootwake: The Fizz That Rewrites Flesh
Rootwake: Frothfather of the World
The Holly Pact: Blood Beneath the Mistletoe
The 2nd Mass Principle: Building Unbreakable Tribes
Web of Wits: A Survival Guide to Encounters with Anasi the Spider (Aunt Nancy)
The Hexbreaking Handbook: Effective Spells to Remove Curses
Pop Alchemy: Transform Your Life One Sip at a Time
The Mason Code: Leading in Unleadable Times
Petosiris and the Fifth Chamber of Thoth
The Ether Seed Within
The Parent of Tomorrow
Petosiris's Pyramid of Perpetual Wealth
Unlearn the World
Grimoire of the Hollow Tongue
Zodiac Weeds: Finding Your Strain Through the Stars
Aquarius Rises in the Bank
The Sugar God's Smile
The Skinclock Reversal: Biohacking the Face of Time
Debtburn: How to Obliterate What You Owe Forever
The Ice Cream Oracle: What Your Cone Says About Your Future
Silence Is Sovereignty: The Power of Being Unreadable
The Wind That Whispers Through Stone
Path of the Four Directions
Doctor Who: The Maestro's Symphony of Endings
Oxygen Grail: Breathing to Undo the Clock
Zodiacal Collapse: When Stars Devour Time
Teachings from the Red Sand Silence
Doctor Who: Omega – The Broken Equation
Memory Wipe Your Past: Start Over Like a MiB

Mitochondria Prime: Ignite the Core of Youth

A Nest of Roaches

Grub from the Galaxy: MiB Recipes You'll Never Forget

Whiskers of Power: Bastet's Guide to Inner Sovereignty

The Gift Must Cost Them: Negotiation Through Unequal Exchange

The Worm Guys' Wealth Code: Hustle Like an Alien

Bug Out: The Edgar Method for Ruthless Goal Setting

Weaving Life with Spiderwoman's Pattern

Doctor Who: The Rani's Renaissance

How to Get a Job (If You're a Puppygirl)

Speak Through Others: The Art of Proxy Power

T-Rex Your Trauma: Reclaim the Power of Your Primal Self

The Black Briefcase: How MiB Stay Wealthy in Silence

The Thirst Beyond Reason: Understanding Diabetes Insipidus From the Inside Out

Backwoods Witchcraft for Billionaires: The Pagan Path from Dirt Roads to Gold Roads

The Moonshine Grimoire: Fermented Spells for Abundance

The Nameless Geometry

The Wraith's Mixtape: Spellcasting with Songs of Sorrow

The Gallifreyan Gentleman: Silent Wealth, Sonic Confidence, and the Doctor's Code of Living

Sugar Water Confidence

Dino Totems: Spirit Guides from Earth's First Gods

Pumpkin Sigils & Ritual Smoke

The Hózhó Compass

The Distortus Discipline – Order from Inner Mutation

Witchcraft for the Cold-Blooded Soul

Moonlight Over the Blessingway

Water, Interrupted: When the Body Forgets How to Hold On

Deformed but Divine: Embracing Your Asymmetry

Hexes in the Henhouse: The Farm Witch's Guide to Power

The Reversed Flame: A Grimoire of Inverted Power

Salt, Cells, and Sanity: Reclaiming Balance with Diabetes Insipidus

King of the Broken: Crowning the Flawed Self

Moonlight Scars: Emo Moon Magick and the Art of Lunar Sorrow

Noose Spells: Magick of the Hanging Rope

The Goth Cathedral: Rituals of the Broken and Beautiful

The Cretaceous Codex: Dino Spirits and Fossil Magick

The Turkey Bones Ritual

Nine Lives of Manifestation: Unlocking Bastet's Reality Codes

Chaos Muscles: Building Strength from Twisted Pain

Emo Blood Magick: The Veins of Power

The 3AM Flood: Nighttime Urination, Sleep Loss, and the DI Spiral

The Silence Between the Stars

The Lemon Method: Sour Your Way to Success

Starlit Sovereign

The Rite of Twelve Gates: Walking the Gates of the Duat.

Cornbread and Conjure: Recipes for Riches and Rootwork

The Black Rose Rituals: Emo Love Spells and Obsession Magick

The Eternal Goodbye: Death Magick and Rebirth Rituals

Sinkrot: The Drain That Remembers

The Hybrid Mindset: Thinking Beyond Evolution

Bone Dry: Navigating Dehydration Before It Breaks You

Wreathcraft: Winter Sigils and Yuletide Spells

The Rite of Twelve Mouths

S'mores of the Damned: Haunted Recipes for Halloween Night

Rethink the Drink: A Beverage Survival Guide for DI Warriors

The Shadow Chord: Guitar Magick and Sonic

Malformed Yet Majestic: Leading When You Feel Wrong Inside

The Cursed Diary: Ink-Stained Spells of the Emo Soul

Anxiety Off Switch: Emergency Reset for a Fried Nervous System

The Energy Heist: How to Take Back Your Life from Drainers

Beyond the Bathroom: Rebuilding Your Social Life With DI

Coyote's Gift for Decision Makers

Ghoul-Goo: Spooky S'mores You'll Die For

Echoes in the Mirror: Scrying and Self-Destruction Magick

Thread and Thorn: Stitching Spells from Rural Cloth

The Mogwai Mind: Building Untouchable Wealth from Small Ideas

Be Your Own Guide: Trust Your Inner Compass

Hormones in Chaos: The Endocrine Puzzle of Diabetes Insipidus

ChronoCleanse: Detox Your Biological Timeline

The Limb You Hide Is the One That Saves You

Leaves, Bones, and Whisper Spells

The Dinosaur Mindset: Prehistoric Tactics for Modern Wealth

Clawing Back Control: A Bastet Method for Boundaries and Empowerment

Samhain Codes of the Forgotten

Orange Alchemy: The Autumnal Spellbook

Monster Within, Master Without

The Sigil That Sleeps

Hearthcraft: Yule Hearth Sigils and Winter Warmth Spells

Temple of the Purring Moon: Rituals from Bastet's Lineage

When the Earth Remembers Your Footsteps

Food for Mood: Eat to Heal Depression, Not Just Survive It

Witch of the Kudzu Vine: Southern Pagan Wealth Secrets

The Invisible Diagnosis: Advocating for Yourself With DI

The Coffin's Lullaby: Sleep Magick and Nightmares as Portals
Ashes of the Will: Rituals for Erasing the Self
The Fracture Rite: Shattering the Magickal Core
Funeral Candles: The Art of Emo Flame Magick
The Black Grimoire: A Blank Ritual for Writing in Absence
Phantom Thirst: A Halloween Survival Guide for Diabetes Insipidus
The Hollow Crown: Emo Royalty and Magick of the Outcast King
Sandpainting for the Soul
Falling Into Balance: Using the Extra Hour to Recalibrate Life
100 Southern Superstitions That Still Work
The DI Child: A Parent's Guide to Raising Hydrated, Happy Kids
The Jungle of Shame: Escaping the Hidden Lab of Doubt
The Witch's Toast: S'mores Spells and Creepy Confections
The Hoodoo Pantry: Spells from the Mason Jar
The Immortal Fortune: Secret Wealth Lessons from Captain Jack Harkness
The Specter's Embrace: Magick for Channeling Ghostly Lovers
Grateful Waters: A Thanksgiving Survival Guide for Diabetes Insipidus
The Seizure Gospel
Harvestbind: Autumn Sigils and Samhain Spells
Doctor Who: The Algorithmic Awakening
Silent Nights, Steady Waters: A Christmas Survival Guide for Diabetes Insipidus
The Extra Hour Effect: How One Hour Can Transform Everything
Blade Between the Breaths
Running with the Mountain Shadows
Echoes of the Failed Experiment – Becoming a Living Legacy

Swamp Witches & River Ghosts: Real Southern Hauntings

Cornbread Prophecies: Magical Recipes from a Southern Table

Doctor Who: The Signal in the Star

Bloomcraft: Spring Sigils and Equinox Enchantments

Vanisher: How to Disappear from the Internet Without Losing Your Life

The Ultimate Christmas Cookie Cookbook

The Unbreakable Parent: How to Mentally Survive Raising Kids in a Broken World

Time Debt: How to Reclaim the Hours You Didn't Know You Lost

One Month, One Million: Unconventional Cash Creation Tactics

Doctor Who: The Cyber Conversion Protocol

Black Friday Frenzy: The Art of Finding Hidden Online Deals

The Grimoire Buried Under the Apple Tree

Digital Couponing Masterclass: Your Step-by-Step Guide to Black Friday Savings

The Fire Inside the Flint

Shadows on the Ceiling: The Emo Guide to Astral Magick

The Bone-Eaters Beneath Us

Black Friday Bundle Blueprint: Creating Irresistible Product Packages for Maximum Sales

Thirteen Nights of Unbinding

Doctor Who: Engines of Influence

Pumpkin Spice Alchemy: Recipes of Fire and Frost

When Raptor Met Rexy: Prehistoric Lessons in Wild Romance

Oblivion's Candle: Burn the Path Behind You

Campfire Curses and Chocolate: A Halloween S'mores Grimoire

Get Some Tarot cards: https://www.makeplayingcards.com/sell/apophis-occult-shop

Get some shirts: https://www.bonfire.com/store/apophis-shirt-emporium/

Instagrams:
@apophis_enterprises,
@apophisbookemporium,
@apophisscardshop
Twitter: @apophisenterpr1
Tiktok:@apophisenterprise
Youtube: @sg1fan23477
Hive: @sg1fan23477
CheeLee: @SG1fan23477

Podcast: Apophis Chat Zone: https://open.spotify.com/show/5zXbrCLEV2xzCp8ybrfHsk?si=fb4d4fdbdce44dec

Newsletter: https://apophiss-newsletter-27c897.beehiiv.com/

If you want to support me or see posts of other projects that I have come over to: **buymeacoffee.com/mpetchinskg**

I post there daily several times a day

Get your Dinowicca or Christmas themed digital products, especially Santa Raptor songs and other musics. Here: **https://sg1fan23477.gumroad.com**

Apophis Yuletide Digital has not only digital Christmas items, but it will have all things with Dinowicca as well as other Digital products.

www.ingramcontent.com/pod-product-compliance
Lightning Source LLC
LaVergne TN
LVHW022020200926
848481LV00007B/2462